GHOSTS

BY NADIA HIGGINS

BELLWETHER MEDIA • MINNEAPOLIS, MN

EPIC BOOKS are no ordinary books. They burst with intense action, high-speed heroics, and shadows of the unknown. Are you ready for an Epic adventure?

This edition first published in 2014 by Bellwether Media, Inc.

No part of this publication may be reproduced in whole or in part without written permission of the publisher. For information regarding permission, write to Bellwether Media, Inc., Attention: Permissions Department, 5357 Penn Avenue South, Minneapolis, MN 55419.

Library of Congress Cataloging-in-Publication Data

Higgins, Nadia.
  Ghosts / by Nadia Higgins.
    pages cm. – (Epic : Unexplained Mysteries)
  Summary: "Engaging images accompany information about ghosts. The combination of high-interest subject matter and light text is intended for students in grades 2 through 7"– Provided by publisher.
  Audience: Ages 7-12.
  Includes bibliographical references and index.
  ISBN 978-1-62617-104-6 (hardcover : alk. paper)
  1. Ghosts–Juvenile literature. I. Title.
  BF1461.H52 2014
  133.1–dc23
                    2013037389

Designed by Jon Eppard.

Printed in the United States of America, North Mankato, MN.

TABLE OF CONTENTS

GUST OR GHOST?

A family checks in to an empty, old hotel. A strange shadow appears outside of their room. It moves toward them but then disappears.

Suddenly, a door creaks open. Then BAM!
It slams shut. But nobody is there. Was that a
gust of wind or a ghost?

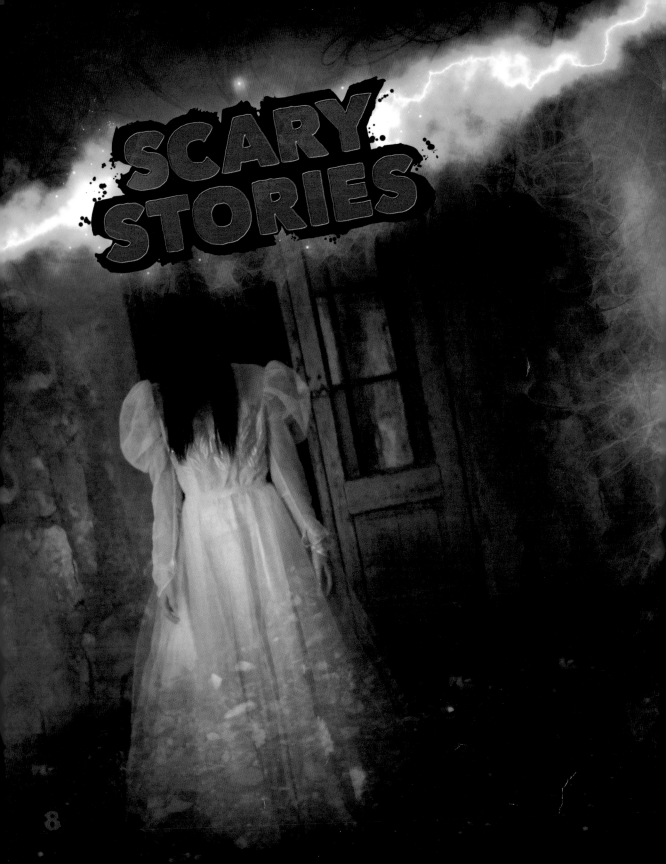

SCARY STORIES

GHOST SHIP

Since the 1700s, there have been stories about a ghost ship called the *Flying Dutchman*. People say this ship was lost in a storm but still sails.

For thousands of years, people around the world have told ghost stories. These stories tell of restless spirits of the dead.

Stories describe different kinds of ghosts. Some haunt their old houses. Other messenger ghosts try to contact their loved ones.

PRESIDENTS' RESIDENCE

Many U.S. presidents are said to still roam the halls of the White House. Abraham Lincoln and Andrew Jackson are among those that people report seeing.

11

Some ghosts scare people for fun. Poltergeists make loud noises and move objects. Sometimes they even push people.

SIGNS OF A POLTERGEIST

- Being pushed or scratched
- Disappearing objects
- Electronics turning on and off by themselves
- Flickering lights
- Objects moving on their own
- Sounds of knocks or footsteps
- Unexplained odors, such as perfume or pipe smoke

EVIDENCE?

Are ghost stories really true? Many people think so. Some point to eerie photos as proof. They say blurry shapes and lights are spirits.

A GHOSTLY SENSE

Psychics are among those who believe in ghosts. They claim they can sense a ghost's energy in a room.

15

Ghost hunters look for restless spirits in old houses and graveyards. They use thermometers, cameras, and voice recorders to search for ghosts.

CHILL OUT
Some people think that a sudden drop in temperature can be a sign of a ghostly visitor.

Skeptics say ghost stories have natural explanations. A drafty window explains a chill. Reflections and tricks of light cause shadows and blurry spots in photos.

TYPES OF GHOSTS

Apparition
A spirit that looks human but does not have flesh

Demon
An evil spirit

Fetch
The spirit of a living person

Mist
A cloudy swirl

Orb
A small ball of light

Poltergeist
A spirit that moves objects and makes noises

Residual
A spirit that appears in one place and does the same action over and over

Shadow
A dark cloud where a normal shadow would not be

Nobody has proven that ghosts exist. However, people continue to tell scary ghost stories. Have you ever seen something you cannot explain?

GLOSSARY

blurry—not clear

creaks—squeaks slowly

drafty—cold because of the movement of cool air

eerie—creepy

messenger ghosts—ghosts that contact loved ones with comforting or warning messages

poltergeists—invisible ghosts that scare people by making noise and moving objects

recorders—small devices that record sounds; ghost hunters use voice recorders to ask questions and capture responses.

reflections—images that are seen on a smooth, shiny surface; a mirror shows the reflection of a person's face.

restless—unable to rest

skeptics—people who doubt the truth of something

TO LEARN MORE

At the Library

Bouvier, Charles. *The Ghost Hunter's Guide*. Mankato, Minn.: Sea-to-Sea Publications, 2012.

Ganeri, Anita. *Ghosts and Other Specters*. New York, N.Y.: PowerKids Press, 2011.

Hamilton, S.L. *Ghosts*. Edina, Minn.: ABDO Pub. Company, 2011.

On the Web

Learning more about ghosts is as easy as 1, 2, 3.

1. Go to www.factsurfer.com.

2. Enter "ghosts" into the search box.

3. Click the "Surf" button and you will see a list of related Web sites.

With factsurfer.com, finding more information is just a click away.

INDEX

The images in this book are reproduced through the courtesy of: Peter Dedeurwaerder/ Jeff Thrower, front cover (composite), pp. 12-13 (composite); clearviewstock/ andreiuc88, pp. 4-5 (composite); Zurijeta, p. 6; kevdog818, p. 7; Lario Tus, p. 8; PLRANG, p. 9; Frontpage/ thatsmymop/ Susan Law Cain, pp. 10-11 (composite); Photopqr/ L'Union de Reims/ Newscom, p. 14 (top); AP Photo/ The Alton Telegraph/ Jim Bowling, p. 14 (bottom); Studio-Annika, p. 15; Greg Wahl-Stephens/ AP Images, p. 16; NBCU Photo Bank/ Getty Images, p. 17; Grischa Georgiew/ TomaB, pp. 18-19 (composite); Meewezen Photography/ ostill, pp. 20-21 (composite).